MARGRET & H.A. REY'S
Curious George
Plants a Tree

Written by Monica Perez
Illustrated in the style of H. A. Rey by Anna Grossnickle Hines

Houghton Mifflin Harcourt
Boston   New York

For Isabel Perez-Reyzin, with love. —M.P.

To all the caretakers of the earth. —A.H.

www.hmhbooks.com

The text of this book is set in Adobe Garamond.
The illustrations are watercolor.

The Library of Congress has cataloged the hardcover edition as follows:
Perez, Monica.
Curious George plants a tree / written by Monica Perez; illustrated in the style of H.A. Rey
by Anna Grossnickle Hines.
p. cm.
Summary: The mischievous monkey learns about protecting the environment by planting
trees and recycling paper. Includes tips on conserving energy and resources.
[1. Environmental protection—Fiction. 2. Recycling (Waste)—Fiction. 3. Trees—Fiction.
4. Monkeys—Fiction.] I. Hines, Anna Grossnickle, ill. II. Rey, H. A. (Hans Augusto),
1898-1977. III. Title.
PZ7.P42583Cv 2009
[E]—dc22
2008037384

ISBN: 978-0-547-15087-1
ISBN: 978-0-547-29776-7 pb

Printed in Malaysia
TWP 10 9 8 7 6 5 4 3 2
4500260490

George was a good little monkey and always very curious. Today was a good day to be curious. The man with the yellow hat was taking George to the science museum.

The museum was one of George's favorite places. There was always something new to see and interesting to learn.

Often there was a special exhibit. George wanted to know what it was today, but first he had to make his favorite museum stops:

the rocket room,

the mirror maze,

and the butterfly space.

Finally, George and his friend made it to the special exhibits room.
The sign read HOW **YOU** CAN TAKE CARE OF OUR PLANET.

George learned many things:

how all people, animals, plants, air, and water on the planet make up the environment,
how trees help keep the air clean,
and how people can help protect the environment from pollution and too much trash.

George had a great time and didn't get into any of his usual mischief.

As he and his friend were leaving,
they bumped into the museum director.

Dr. Lee looked happy to see him.

"How is my best monkey visitor?" Dr. Lee asked George. "I'm so glad I ran into you. I wanted to tell you that we're having a Green Day rally tomorrow at the park."

George was curious—whatever a rally was, he was sure that the park was a good place to do it.

"We're going to plant a truckload of trees and collect used paper for recycling," Dr. Lee explained. "We didn't have much time to advertise, but we need lots of volunteers. How would you like to help out?"

There was nothing that George liked better than to help.

"What a great idea!" the man agreed. "We'll be there."

That night George was ready to do his part for the recycling drive. He gathered every newspaper in the house. He stacked old mail on top of the papers. He piled empty cardboard boxes and food cartons on top of that. What a heap!

What more could he add? George scratched his head.
Then he took several books off his bedroom shelf.

Just as George was about to add them to his recycling pile, someone lifted the books out of his hands.

"Not so fast, George," the man said. "These books are made of paper all right, but you can read and enjoy them many times. And when you're done, you can donate them to other kids or your library. Reusing is just as important as recycling."

The next morning
George and his friend set
out for the park with their
wagon of neatly stacked paper.
Suddenly the man stopped and said,
"I forgot my gardening gloves! Go on
without me, George. I'll be there soon."

As George walked down the street, he spotted
several newspapers lying about on his neighbors' front
stoops. George had an idea. He had lots of room in his
wagon. He could recycle all those newspapers.

And the newspapers were not the only things he could recycle. He noticed a stack of paper cups sitting on a table under a tree. Into the wagon they went!

So did a pile of magazines.

And a heap of papers someone left on the sidewalk.

George was happy with his great load. At the park he found Dr. Lee already hard at work.

"Good morning, George," Dr. Lee said. "I'm so glad you came and brought all your friends. We need lots of help to get the job done."

George turned around. He was surprised to see
so many faces, but they did not look very helpful.
They looked angry!

The man with the yellow hat arrived just in time. He explained to their neighbors that George was gathering paper for a good cause. They were no longer mad. They even stayed to help plant the trees.

"George, you saved our Green Day!" Dr. Lee said, with gratitude. "These trees will provide fresher air. And each summer we'll have more shade, which means we'll use less water to keep the grass green. Thank you."

Being a monkey, George had known all along how important trees were.